My HOLY HOUR
Our Lady of Mount Carmel

A Devotional Journal

Season: _____
Date: _____

Belongs to: _____

My Holy Hour - Our Lady of Mount Carmel is part of the *My Holy Hour Devotional Journal Series*. While all journals will have some similar structure and intent, each one will have minor changes to make it unique. Cover image depicts the painting Our Lady of Mount Carmel (19th century) by Raimundo da Costa e Silva and is located in the National Museum of Fine Arts in Rio de Janeiro, Brazil.

Go to our website for a free copy of

How to Use a Prayer Journal during Holy Hour
www.HolyHourBooks.com

Holy Hour Books
P.O. Box 430577
Houston, TX 77243

My Holy Hour Devotional Journals

ISBN-13: 978-1-725584-71-6
ISBN-10: 1-725584-71-9

First Printing: 2018

Holy Hour Books is an imprint of Ordinary Matters Publishing.

Printed in the United States of America

O most beautiful Flower of Mount Carmel, fruitful vine, splendor of Heaven, Blessed Mother of the Son of God, Immaculate Virgin, assist me in this my necessity. (Insert need) O Star of the Sea, help me and show me herein that you are my Mother.

O Holy Mary, Mother of God, Queen of Heaven and earth, I humbly beseech you from the bottom of my heart, to succor me in this my necessity. There are none that can withstand your power. O show me herein that you are my Mother.

O Mary, conceived without sin, pray for us that have recourse to thee. (Repeat 3x) Sweet Mother, I place this cause in your hands. (Repeat 3x)

— Novena Prayer to Our Lady of Mount Carmel (Flower of Carmel)

Why Keep a Holy Hour

"First, the Holy Hour is not a devotion; it is a sharing in the work of redemption... our Lord asked: 'Could you not watch one hour with Me?'. In other words, he asked for an hour of reparation to combat the hour of evil; an hour of victimal union with the Cross to overcome the anti-love of sin.

Secondly, the only time Our Lord asked the Apostles for anything was the night he went into his agony... As often in the history of the Church since that time, evil was awake, but the disciples were asleep. That is why there came out of His anguished and lonely Heart the sigh: 'Could you not watch one hour with me?' Not for an hour of activity did He plead, but for an hour of companionship.

The third reason I keep up the Holy Hour is to grow more and more into his likeness. As Paul puts it: 'We are transfigured into his likeness, from splendor to splendor.' We become like that which we gaze upon. Looking into a sunset, the face takes on a golden glow. Looking at the Eucharistic Lord for an hour transforms the heart in a mysterious way as the face of Moses was transformed after his companionship with God on the mountain. Something happens to us similar to that which happened to the disciples at Emmaus. On Easter Sunday afternoon when the Lord met them, he asked why they were so gloomy. After spending some time in his presence, and hearing again the secret of spirituality - The Son of Man must suffer to enter into his Glory'" - their time with him ended and their "hearts were on fire." — Bishop Fulton Sheen

My Holy Hour

How to Keep a Holy Hour

"I have found that it takes some time to catch fire in prayer. This has been one of the advantages of the daily Hour. It is not so brief as to prevent the soul from collecting itself and shaking off the multitudinous distractions of the world. Sitting before the Presence is like a body exposing itself before the sun to absorb its rays. Silence in the Hour is a tete-a-tete with the Lord. In those moments, one does not so much pour out written prayers, but listening takes its place. We do not say: 'Listen, Lord, for Thy servant speaks,' but 'Speak, Lord, for Thy servant heareth.'"— Bishop Fulton Sheen

"Know also that you will probably gain more by praying fifteen minutes before the Blessed Sacrament than by all the other spiritual exercises of the day. True, Our Lord hears our prayers anywhere, for He has made the promise, 'Ask, and you shall receive,' but He has revealed to His servants that those who visit Him in the Blessed Sacrament will obtain a more abundant measure of grace."— St. Alphonsus Liguori

Holy Hour Pages

"The purpose of the Holy Hour is to encourage deep personal encounter with Christ."

— *Bishop Fulton Sheen*

My Holy Hour

My Holy Hour

My Holy Hour

61

My Holy Hour

HOLY HOUR QUOTES

"Mary has the authority over the angels and the blessed in heaven. As a reward for her great humility, God gave her the power and mission of assigning to saints the thrones made vacant by the apostate angels who fell away through pride. Such is the will of the almighty God who exalts the humble, that the powers of heaven, earth and hell, willingly or unwillingly, must obey the commands of the humble Virgin Mary. For God has made her queen of heaven and earth, leader of his armies, keeper of his treasure, dispenser of his graces, mediatrix on behalf of men, destroyer of his enemies, and faithful associate in his great works and triumphs."

— St. Louis de Montfort

O beautiful Flower of Carmel, most fruitful Vine, Splendor of Heaven, holy and singular, who brought forth the Son o God, still ever remaining a Pure Virgin, assist me in this necessity. (Insert your need) O Star of the Sea, help and protect me! Show me that thou art my Mother.

O Mary, Conceived without sin, pray for us who have recourse to thee. Mother and Ornament of Carmel, pray for us! Virgin, Flower of Carmel, pray for us. Hope of all who die wearing the Scapular, pray for us.

St. Joseph, Friend of the Sacred Heart, pray for us. St. Joseph, Chaste Spouse of Mary, pray for us. St. Joseph, our Patron, pray for us. O sweet Heart of Mary, be my salvation!

— Flos Carmeli Prayer to Blessed Mother by St Simon Stock

Record Your Favorite Quotes Here

My Holy Hour

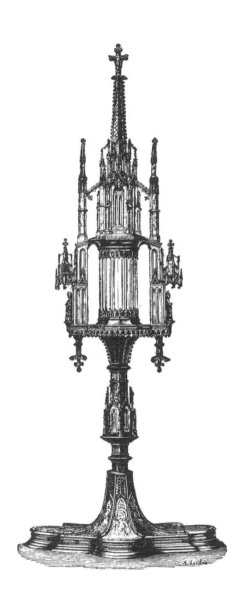

REFLECTIONS

Personal Index

_____ *Pgs* ____

_____ *Pgs* ____

_____ *Pgs* ____

_____ *Pgs* ____

_____ *Pgs* ____

_____ *Pgs* ____

_____ *Pgs* ____

_____ *Pgs* ____

_____ *Pgs* ____

_____ *Pgs* ____

Pgs ____

_____ *Pgs* ____

_____ *Pgs* ____

_____ *Pgs* ____

_____ *Pgs* ____

_____ *Pgs* ____

_____ *Pgs* ____

_____ *Pgs* ____

_____ *Pgs* ____

_____ *Pgs* ____

_____ *Pgs* ____

_____ *Pgs* ____

_____ *Pgs* ____

HOLY HOUR JOURNALS

Thank you for your interest in *Holy Hour Journals*. Discover more about using journals to deepen your prayer life by going to our website and getting a free copy of

How to Use a Prayer Journal during Holy Hour
www.HolyHourBooks.com

The Holy Hour Devotional Journal Series has been created to help Catholics from all walks of life to discover, explore, and enjoy the many rewards from a deeper connection to Christ.

Like our Facebook Page:
https://www.facebook.com/HolyHourBooks

Made in the USA
Middletown, DE
29 July 2023

35920266R00078